IMAGES OF ENGLAND

OFFERTON

IMAGES OF ENGLAND

OFFERTON

RAY PRESTON

TEMPUS

Frontispiece: An interesting photograph of a group of local people, who have gathered to watch this rare sight of a photographer and all his equipment.

First published 2005

Tempus Publishing Limited
The Mill, Brimscombe Port,
Stroud, Gloucestershire, GL5 2QG
www.tempus-publishing.com

British Library Cataloguing in Publication Data.
A catalogue record for this book is available from the British Library.

ISBN 0 7524 3450 0

Typesetting and origination by Tempus Publishing Limited.
Printed in Great Britain.

Contents

Acknowledgements   6

Introduction   7

one   Roads   9

two   Public Houses & Businesses   33

three Houses   51

four   Churches, Schools & Events   85

five   Farms   107

six   Views   117

Acknowledgements

My thanks go to various people and organisations for their permission to use many of the new photographs in this book. They are, namely: David Reid, Stockport Archive Library, the *Stockport Express Advertiser and Times*, Eamon O'Niel, Granada Television, Ernest Neild, Mrs Cairns, Harry Lees and John Turner.

Introduction

Having lived in Offerton for over sixty-five years, I feel reasonably competent to relate a little of the knowledge of the place which I have picked up over the years.

As with a number of Cheshire villages, Offerton has virtually doubled in size. The old boundaries have spread both to the north and west. When I came here in 1936, ribbon development had begun by following the one major road which had run through the village for over 500 years. That was the road we now know as the Marple Road. Samuel Oldknow, the Marple and Mellor mill owner, had built a turnpike road from the boundary of Marple village at Dan Bank along an old pack-horse trail to the Offerton Fold. This was opened in 1797. At that time the whole of Offerton was a web of linking farm tracks. Many of these formed the basis for the roads we have today. Lisburn Lane linked to Great Moor, Offerton Lane to Littlemoor. The oldest, Bongs Lane, probably dates back over 1,000 years. Bongs is actually the Anglo-Saxon word for bones. This path comes up from a ford over the Goyt called Broadford, rising steeply and progressing across Bean Leach. Then, crossing a bridge called Saltersbrugge★ (long since disappeared), having traversed Haverford Walks, passes into Hazel Grove at what is now the rear of the Royal Oak pub.

Ann Cross, local historian from the 1960s, took a great interest in the history of Offerton and published a small book on some of her discoveries. Without doubt Ann's greatest achievement was the discovery of a link between the Dodge family of America and the Dodges of Cheshire, and, more importantly, the Dodges of Offerton.

This village has now spread further than I could ever have imagined. Today we accept as part of Offerton, Littlemoor, Mile End Lane, Woodbank, Vernon Park and Spring Gardens. The only sad part of this so-called progress is the fact that we have lost almost all of our historically important buildings. Fortunately we can illustrate through the power of photography what we have lost to the developers.

Despite the fact that I was born a Lancashire lad, I am proud of my long association with the Cheshire landscape.

Ray Preston

* Saltersbrugge (Anglo-Saxon?), salters bridge, so named after a packhorse trail for salt-carrying pack animals.

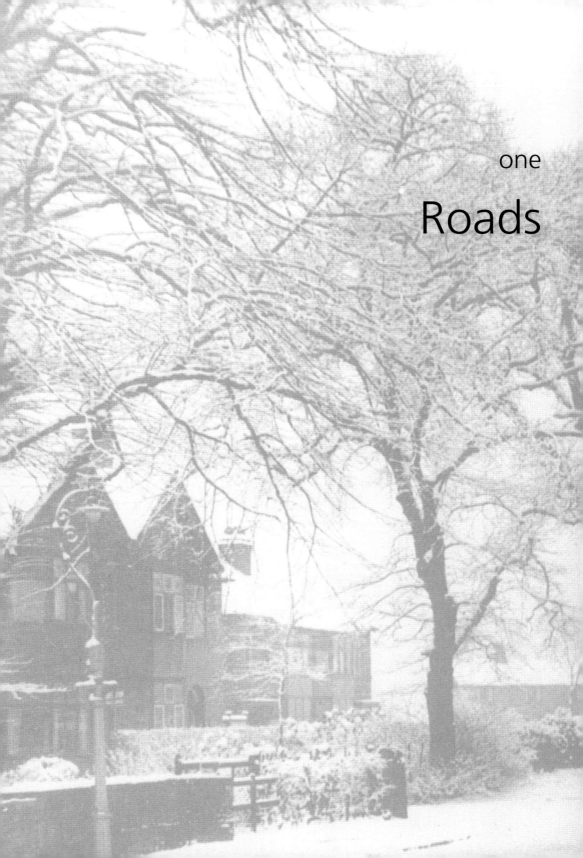

one

Roads

The toll house built by the Marple and Mellor mill owner Samuel Oldknow in 1797. This building stood at the corner of Marple Road and Dooley Lane until 1922, when road widening took place.

Unfortunately, the fact that the toll house stood on the brink of a steep drop into the Torkington Brook necessitated its demolition.

In 1949 I was given an old Kodak box camera which gave me the opportunity to take some photographs that are now historically very interesting. Here on the right we can see a lorry carrying milk churns, plus the North-Western buses to and from Marple.

There was at one time a regular collapse of the Marple Road close to Dooley Lane due to a natural spring running off the opposite bank. The young rider in the photograph is one of the sons of Henry Hough-Wilson of Jessiefields.

In this postcard the open-topped bus stands at the junction of Offerton Road and Marple Road. The house on the right is the aptly named Seventeen Windows and the road running to the right was to Bosden or Hazel Grove.

Opposite above: This photograph shows the last of the Oldknow fence posts standing on the Offerton side of the boundary.

Opposite below: In this photograph the Edwardian lady awaits the bus in front of the Seventeen Windows, on what was originally called the turnpike road.

Opposite: The line of the old packhorse trail is built up today on either side. It is named Marple Old Road.

Right: The rough path, still used today, is part of the network of packhorse trails which criss-crossed Offerton and date back over 500 years. Due to the steepness of the incline here, Samuel Oldknow decided to bypass to the right when he turnpiked the road in 1797, a detour of about 200 yards.

Below: The diverted Marple Road, seen here during winter, still shows an access driveway entrance on the right to a Victorian house called Jessiefields.

The Marple Road. Stone walls and steep roads typify Offerton and form part of its character, farms and historic houses abounding on either side.

This very old photograph shows the village green rough and unkempt. The opening between the farm and the houses is named Bongs Lane and joins a ford crossing the River Goyt deep in the Bongs Valley. Rumour has it that the route was followed from the Roman fortress at Melandra Castle through to Mancunia.

Marple Road sweeps down to its lowest point above the Fogg Brook, today called the Poise Brook. The Foggbrook Mill, demolished in 2004, can be seen on the bend.

The Foggbrook bridge, built to take the turnpike road in 1797, was put in place by the stonemasons who carved the bridges and walls along the Marple canals.

Holiday Lane in the Gnat Hole is miss spelt; back in the early 1900s it should have been named Halliday Lane as it runs up to the famous Halliday Hill Farm. The East Cheshire drag hounds used the area down to the River Goyt.

A small community of people have lived in the Gnat Hole for hundreds of years, certainly since the fifteenth century.

This is obviously a wartime photograph with the concrete blocks ready to roll into the road in case of enemy tanks invading. The advertisement on the wall of the smithy at the junction of Holiday Lane and Marple Road is for the ATS.

This winter scene is taken from an 8mm cine film frame. The steep slope running down to the bridge, the smithy and the adjoining sweet shop are long since gone.

A North-Western 813 Dennis double-decker bus negotiates the hill towards Stockport High. Despite the hawthorn hedges on either side, sitting on the top deck allows a view of the Offerton Sand and Gravel workings in the background.

The crest of the hill where Ormes Farm used to stand. The driveway through the five-bar gate to the left is used today to access Mellor Court.

Above and below: These scenes depict the Marple Road at different seasons of the year. Above, early autumn has arrived, while below sees the road in mid-winter, with a low, golden sun picking out the skeletons of trees along Marple Road.

Beautifully layered hawthorn hedges run along the roadside towards Brookside Farm. The opening on the right is the driveway to Offerton Hall Farm, later to be named Old Hall Drive. Note the old bus stop sign on the lamp post.

A lovely snowy scene of Marple Road going north towards Stockport. 1920s semi-detached houses are on the left, with a farm and then a group of very old buildings on the bend opposite Chadwell Road.

The as yet unbuilt Lisburn Lane at the junction with Marple Road. This dates the photograph to just after the Second World War. A large hoarding on the future site of the Golden Hind advertises building land. The Dodgefold cottages are still standing in the background.

Lisburn Lane could only boast a few houses at the eastern end of the lane until after the Second World War. Up to the early 1900s, the lane had dog-legged to the right by the old pear tree through a fold of farm cottages called Dodgefold. The lane continued on to Dialstone Lane.

The mid-section of the old Lisburn Lane is typical of an old farm lane dating back hundreds of years and serving the various farming communities. Dialstone Central School on the left was built on the edge of the countryside. Stiles still accessed many pathways to Marple, Hazel Grove and Romiley.

The old car and the lack of garden walls seen here date this postcard to the late 1920s.

The end of Offerton Lane. Victorian houses can be seen on the right, with the Gardeners Arms and the old church standing at the junction of Banks Lane and Hall Street.

Looking towards the Union Chapel, the three roads converging are Banks Lane, Offerton Lane and Hall Street. The church has now been demolished and the ground has been utilized for the pub car park.

Above and below: Two photographs showing the old and the modern Bean Leach Road. The top photograph shows how it was in 1936 and the one below how it looks more recently. The cobbles have been covered over, the road straightened and the farm demolished, but the tree still stands at the Shearwater Road junction. In the old photograph can be seen the Victorian Highfield House on the left and the builders constructing Pychley House in the distance.

Again roads converge, namely Hempshaw Lane, Dialstone Lane and Banks Lane. The Victorian FingerPost Hotel building replaced an old cottage beer house in 1906.

Dialstone Lane, previously called Black Lane, fades into the distance. On the extreme left can be seen the Industrial School for Girls.

An idyllic picture of Mile End Lane in the autumn. Prestigious houses spread the length of this lane, while the high brick wall bordered the historic Mile End Hall.

A postcard of a carriage and pair making its way down Torkington Lane, possibly en route to the railway station at Hazel Grove for the occupants to take a trip into Manchester.

A colour postcard of Dooley Lane depicting the Hare and Hounds, before the re-alignment of the lane.

Close by the Otterspool Bridge runs Mill Lane, which follows the River Goyt for approximately 500 yards. A leat had been dug in readiness for a water-powered mill at the end of the lane but it was never built.

Hall Street runs down into the town of Stockport. The street has remained virtually unchanged since Victorian times, with the pub still standing to the left and the houses and the shops still there. The only object not seen today is the electric bus.

Cherry Tree Lane joins two major roads, Buxton Road, which is the main A6, and Dialstone Lane. History books relate that the last gibbet stood on the corner of this junction.

This very rare picture postcard shows the old toll house at the end of The Fold. As no water tower can be seen on the hat works, this photograph has to be pre-1906.

This narrow exit onto Marple Road existed until the 1970s, when the increase in traffic necessitated a new and wider junction. This was achieved by re-siting the exit on the north side of the Wrights Arms. This 1935 photograph shows a concrete phone box and the site cabin of the then sand quarry owner, Thomas Whitely.

Finally, at the end of this chapter on roads I have included this tiny footbridge known as Donkey Bridge in Kays Wood. Crossing the Torkington Brook deep in the wood, this path is part of the Cown Edge Way. In my youth I frequently used this bridge after crossing Yew Tree farmland whilst heading up toward Hawk Green.

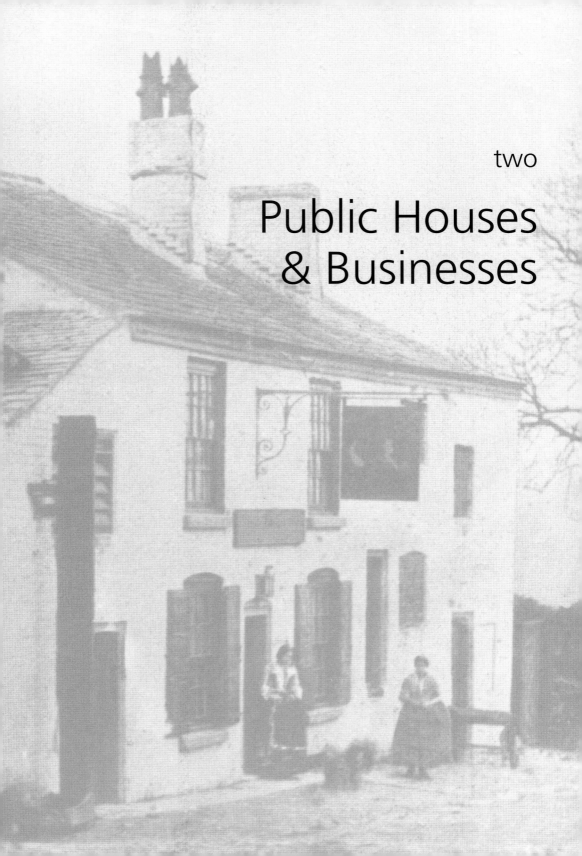

two

Public Houses
& Businesses

This photograph of the Wrights Arms is without doubt the oldest picture to appear in this book. Taken from a glass plate negative held by Stockport Archive Library dated very early 1800s, the inn was originally opened in 1756 by Ann Richardson and in later years the licensee was Lucy Paulden, who I think is the lady in the photograph along with her daughter.

Originally named the Foggbrook Inn, early modification to the Wrights Arms included the removal of a thatched roof and the addition of two dormers. At the time of this photograph, the Bean Leach Road exit was on the left of the building.

In 1935 the Wrights Arms was still very much isolated, standing alone at the corner of the Marple and Bean Leach Roads.

A pseudo black and white timber façade finishes the twentieth-century modifications to the Wrights Arms. Today its modern appearance belies its ancient lineage. Here the new Bean Leach Road is just being dug out.

The modern-day appearance of the Strawberry Gardens has changed very little from its early beginnings in the 1700s, when it was a tiny beer house encouraging soldiers from the nearby Victoria Barracks on Hall Street to bring their girlfriends to dance on the special dancing boards. Families were also encouraged to bring their children to pick the ripe strawberries grown in the gardens at the back.

The Strawberry Gardens.

The aptly named Finger Post directed travellers to their various destinations, usually after they had partaken of a beverage. Here the tiny beer house customers spill out onto the front for a photograph.

A day trip from the rebuilt Victorian public house. Bells Brewery was a local firm owned by Henry Bell, Mayor of Stockport, in 1906. His brewery was situated farther down Hempshaw Lane. This brewery straddled the Hempshaw Brook and water for brewing was drawn from deep boreholes in the sandstone rock.

The Stag and Pheasant Inn. This beautiful stone and flagg-roofed cottage, along with a barn, both back onto the River Goyt, which is spanned by a busy road over the Otterspool Bridge. No doubt many thirsty passers-by would call in to quench their thirst here.

The Stag and Pheasant Inn is now a family home, and the old barn has been beautifully modernized for residents to live in lavish comfort. There are spectacular views all around the two houses.

The Midway, yet another beer house along the Marple Road and an obvious re-build from its original humble beginnings. The original date stone, re-sited in the gable end of the house, featured a capital D, so we can be fairly certain that someone of the Dodge family would have been the resident. An interesting point in the history of this popular pub was that it only ever held a license to sell beer, but not spirits.

Many regulars were sorry to see the demise of this building, and a little of its humble beginnings were exposed when demolition began – the hand-hewn beams in the roof were obviously original.

Offerton Sand and Gravel works. In the early 1920s, Thomas Whitely of Windy Ridge Farm discovered a deposit of glacial sand and gravel. Needing some sand for a concreting job on the farm, he proceeded to dig in the area of the deposit. It was only then that he realized what a massive amount there was underground; thousands of tons of beautiful sea-washed gravel ready for grading. Working from a tiny brick office, which still exists today, Tom and his son set up a business which still thrives.

At this petrol station pumps originally set up for fuelling the lorries on site soon became open for public sales. Selling Shell and Benzole, this is another business that still thrives today, although on a much larger scale.

This broad landscape photograph taken from Bean Leach Road in 1936 covers a lot of interesting detail. Beginning at the extreme right-hand side it shows 'Old Farm'. Moving left, a pair of semi-detached houses and the seventeenth century Ridge Cottages situated on the edge of the village green. The Wright's Arms is to the left of the road and then the broad expanse of the Offerton Sand and Gravel Quarry. The face of the quarry is clearly seen but more important is the only photographic evidence of the massive pebble grading machine that we have. Through the 1940s, this grader rattled thousands of tons of sea-washed pebbles from conveyer belts into various sizes for distribution. These deposits of gravel had been left from an ice-age glacier twelve million years ago.

A photograph showing the Foggbrook Mill shortly before demolition began in 2003.

Opposite above: The Foggbrook Mill was historically a hidden gem only revealed 200 years later when it was being demolished. Built originally in the late 1700s by William Lavender, with the intention of opening a cotton mill, this ultimately proved fruitless due to a slump in the cotton industry. The original plan was to harness water power from the Fogg Brook and a large reservoir was dug for reserve water power. Some years later the mill was sold to Thomas Wilson, who began a bleaching and dyeing industry. This is another Kodak box camera photograph taken in 1950 by the author. Note the fishermen at the edge of the reservoir.

Opposite below: This photograph in about 1925 depicts dyeing and bleaching, with clouds of steam rising from the buildings. The dutch barn is well-stocked with hay to feed the horses that were used to pull the heavy drays,

The grand opening of the community project took place on 23 April 1994. The ceremony was conducted by the Mayor of Stockport, Cllr Philip Harrison, accompanied by the Lady Mayoress, Mrs Harrison. In the foreground stand the author and his wife, Muriel Preston.

Opposite above: In the winter of 1990, the local community council offered to clean up a derelict eyesore on the site of the Foggbrook Mill. The mill stream had the potential for being a beauty spot to be enjoyed by the general public.

Opposite below: During the general work in the Poise Brook, a millstone was uncovered and the River Board raised it from the bed of the stream.

In 2002 the mill was closed down and the land sold for a housing development. Demolition of the mill began in 2003.

The open end to the two storeys of the building expose the steel roof trusses which replaced original wooden beams which had been badly damaged in a suspected arson attack.

As the main building is removed, a 20ft-deep wheel pit is exposed. Advertisments in the *Manchester Mercury* dated 1812 mention a waterwheel with a 24ft fall. This had been a mid-shot wheel, another rarity, taking water into buckets rather than paddles.

In the wheel pit, brick-vaulted cellars are revealed going out under what had been our civic garden area. Dye-stained walls indicate the many pollutants – paper sacks filled with vulcan black, brilliant chrome yellow, madder red and cyan blue – all banned substances, that had lain there for over fifty years to my knowledge.

More vaulted cellars lead towards the stream. Presumably the water from the wheel pit flowed back into the stream. Interesting strata layers depict eras over the last century. The top is a layer of coarse sand on a lime-stone chipping base, the civic garden base. Below is rough brick on laid brick and finally rough crushed mortar and brick.

Massive natural stones were brought to the surface. These had acted as beds for the massive Watts & Boulton steam engines which were brought in when water power was eventually dispensed with. Experts maintain that this mill was the earliest in the town to utilize steam power in about 1830.

Above and below: The Battersby family had a thriving business in Stockport with a fine factory in Offerton. Their family home 'Strathclyde', on Offerton Lane, eventually became an orphanage. A disastrous fire gutted the Battersby hat works in 1906 but the building was saved and afterwards a tall water tower was added to the building, altering the Offerton skyline.

The Curzon Cinema, opened in June 1937, was the first cinema in Offerton and was situated on Turncroft Lane, backing onto Woodbank Park. The programme for the grand opening stated that the manager was Mr J. Wooley. I have many fond memories of attending the Saturday matinee for the weekly serial. Mr Wooley would parade up and down the aisles ejecting any rowdy or boisterous boys. Closing in the 1960s, the cinema became the Palace Theatre Club. This was hosted by the very popular Donald Peers, his radio programme was regularly featured opening with Donald singing his signature tune, *By a Babbling Brook*. The club's claim to fame years later was that a very young quartet called The Beatles had appeared there in the 1960s. In later years it reopened as Hamiltons, a nightclub. There was continued local opposition for many reasons and the building closed, never to reopen, and demolition followed.

Built between Castle Farm Lane and Sandhurst Road in 1936, the Blue Lagoon was an ideal leisure spot and very popular during the early wartime years. Summers seemed more dependable back in the early 1940s. This wonderful pool was the last word in opulence. There was a 30ft-high diving board, water chutes and a gushing fountain of water at the shallow end. Part of the area was marshland and this was capitalized upon. Paddle boats were brought in. The area was very much like the everglades, with numerous small islands which we would land on and claim as our territory. These were halcyon days of glorious sunshine until the late 1940s since when weather patterns seem to have changed!

three

Houses

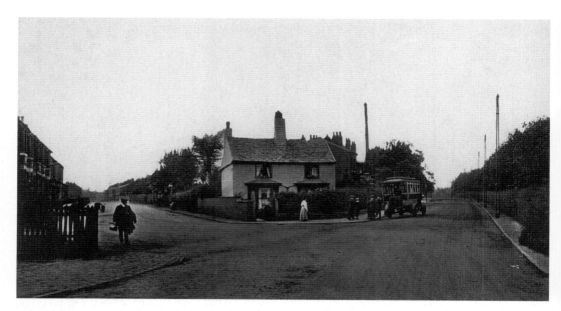

The North Toll House. This beautiful little cottage at the Stockport end of the turnpike was operated and occupied by the Hooley family. The electric bus utilized The Fold as the terminus.

Built in the early 1700s, these five houses, with a communal cellar, served as the workroom for a thriving cottage industry. There are only four of the original houses left today as the end one was badly damaged by a bomb blast during the Second World War.

A pair of fine detached Victorian houses, their original grounds rapidly disappearing as generally they had large kitchen gardens. This gave developers the chance to capitalize on the extensive grounds for smaller properties.

The Hollies, a semi-detached for most of its lifetime. With the demand for care homes for the elderly, this house became a comfortable and well-appointed rest home for many people to enjoy their twilight years.

Lymefield was run for many years as a prestigious private school, where places were eagerly sought after if your family could afford it. A high standard of education was guaranteed by the two maiden ladies, the Misses Lee, who taught at Lymefield. The school was later converted into flats before eventually being demolished.

Opposite above: Samuel Dodge was a weaver in one of the Sundial Cottages. Nail holes in the beams in some rooms show where the looms were fastened and history books inform us of the sundial which was fastened to the chimney. A Latin inscription read *Ad Haec Memento Pendat Eternas*, which we are led to believe translates means, 'On this Moment Hangs Eternity'.

Opposite below: Dodgefold (Thornhill Estate). Groups of farmhouses built in close proximity were typical of the fifteenth and sixteenth centuries. These houses were knocked down in the 1800s and the only record we have is a drawing by the historian John Owen who travelled the length and breadth of Cheshire to record the many fine buildings he saw on his travels. They actually stood where Offerton Drive meets the old Lisburn Lane.

The date stone in the wall states 1751 with the initials R and H. The R stands for Richard Yeardsley, who was a blacksmith. He eventually moved to Marple Bridge.

Opposite above: Over the years of progress many odd buildings were built along the Marple Road, not least this pair of terraced properties on the very edge of the road. Dating from the late nineteenth century with typical sash windows, they have interesting gable ends with Welsh slate protection from the prevailing bad weather.

Opposite below: This photograph shows the sad demise of both houses.

Left: The date stone was preserved after demolition of the house. The H on the stone is probably the initial of Richard Yeardsley's wife.

Below: Built in 1822 originally as a Methodist Sunday school and reading room, Brookdale Cottage was angled away from the Marple Road so that the east end (the altar end), would face the east. This was the norm for most houses of religion. Eventually the building became redundant when the new church was built in 1887. The Sunday school occupied the top floor and the lower area was the living quarters. The schoolroom was accessed by a flight of stone steps.

The Dodge family have lived in Halliday Hill House for over 400 years. They took an active part in the running of the community, occupying the mayoral office on occasion and were signatories on many official documents. The family have become known across the world, particularly in the United States where a member of the Dodge family founded Fort Dodge which eventually became Dodge City.   The view across the wooded valley under thaw shows an extension to the house on the left, which was added in the 1600s.

Probably the most published photograph of Halliday Hill House, taken shortly after the sandstone plinth was cleaned around the base of the building.

An excursion into the loft of Halliday Hill House in search of the elusive cruck frame revealed a floored and plastered room at the east gable end.

The cruck, dating from 1400, but what purpose the tiny room? The 1841 census stated that Sarah Dodge was a maidservant at the house, so in all probability she slept in this room.

Beneath the dog-leg staircase, seventeenth-century wattle and daub and early plasterwork is exposed.

Hand-carved laths used to support the plaster ceiling were exposed during the 1970s.

The twin extensions dating from the mid-sixteenth century protect the staircase built at the same time. Kerridge flagg also succeeded thatch on the roof.

The Mountfield family occupied the house during the 1920s. Alterations were made to the front by replacing a Victorian sash window with a French window.

The newel post and banister dates back to the seventeenth century, while the box framework is typical of cottages.

The withdrawing room boasts beautiful stone mullion windows and rare hand-fashioned window catches are found on the windows both upstairs and downstairs.

This rare Velox snapshot was taken from the rear of Brookdale Cottage looking out over the Gnat Hole. Brookside Cottages can be seen to the left with the Revd Henry Wright's house central. An interesting horse-drawn carriage stands in the field, a former ambulance from the First World War. A burnt-out barn to the right was stuck by lightning many years before.

Above and below: The old postcard above shows the eighteenth-century Ridge Cottages complete with the end extension built at the expense of Mrs Bradshaw-Isherwood of Marple Hall. This was a community hall built for local people to meet and enjoy themselves. Lantern slide shows and lectures were held until a speaker was injured by a falling beam. After this it seemed that nobody would take on the responsibility for the upkeep of the hall and therefore it had to be demolished (see below).

This tiny cottage is the oldest building on the Offerton village green, precariously perched on the edge of the high slope above the Bong Valley. The rear of the house is partially built of stone. On very early maps the house was called Wood Cottage. Today the Victorian gateposts state that it is called Ivy Cottage.

Opposite above: Mount Pleasant is flanked to the right by a Victorian house. The centre cottage of the three is the oldest – with its hood-moulded windows, experts maintain it predates the other two by some 250 years.

Opposite below: The Victorian house itself boasts the ghost of a Roman soldier, seen on numerous occasions by the resident either in the kitchen or the hallway. The story was featured on television many years ago and thanks to its magic a picture can be shown.

Above and below: Many years ago a brick-lined well was discovered in the garden, which may have quenched the thirst of travellers as far back as Roman times.

This group of cottages appears to be a mix of ordinary workers' houses, but one has a more prestigious background (see below).

Holmleigh, apart from a small Victorian addition at the right-hand side, is dated 1697 on its gable end. The obvious grandeur and quality of the handmade brick gives the whole structure a touch of class. This is not the abode of a humble farm worker. A superb piece of ornate plasterwork in a rear bedroom festooned with Tudor roses, oak leaves and acorns suggests a much earlier period than the seventeenth century. A spice cupboard by the fireplace was dated by experts as fifteenth century, possibly reused, but some day we may learn of a more prestigious ownership. History books record that the Macclesfield forest ran down to the River Goyt at Otterspool in Offerton.

The beautiful plasterwork from Holmleigh.

Shady Oak and Offerton Mount, two more cottages teetering on the edge of the Bong Valley. Shady Oak on the left of the picture has a date stone 1801 and has something of a chequered history. Over the years it has been used as both a girls school and a doss house for passing tramps. It was then purchased in a derelict state by Alice Foulds, the widow of a royal dispenser, who wanted to return to Offerton, which was her place of birth.

Jessiefields, a magnificent early Victorian house oozing opulence and stately grandeur. Henry Hough-Wilson, a wealthy flour merchant from Hyde, brought up a large family here. At one end of the house was an elegant glass conservatory. To the left can be seen a large paddock for his horses surrounded by a well-kept hawthorn hedge.

Jessiefields in close-up.

Hough-Wilson pauses at the ornate porchway entrance to Jessiefields whilst his top-hatted coachman Gee steadies the horse.

A young Eric Hough-Wilson astride his Sunbeam motorcycle whilst home on leave during the First World War. He is no doubt going for a spin around the leafy lanes of Offerton.

Eric takes a different mode of transport around the fields.

This opening to the big house can still be seen today leaving the Marple Road, although gone unfortunately are the beautiful ornate gates and the gas lamps.

A proud Henry Hough-Wilson stands with his wife, four daughters and two sons in the garden. Eric, their elder brother is standing at the rear. The font Henry leans on is reputed to have come from a Poynton church.

Sycamore House and Nab Wood Cottage: the old and the new standing in several acres of woodland named Nab Wood. Sycamore House, with it pseudo-Tudor look, is in contrast to the modern bungalow built by the farming family the Masseys, who have farmed in this area for many generations.

One of the prettiest local landmarks, Seventeen Windows stands at the junction of Offerton Road and Marple Road, a surviving reminder of a cottage industry dating back to the mid-1700s. The seventeen tiny windows in the roof space enabled the community cottagers to work together at their looms in relative comfort with sufficient light to see. A very young yew tree can be seen to the right growing in the garden of Yew Tree Farm.

In 1944 Seventeen Windows suffered a disastrous fire. The eastern end of the building was destroyed with the loss of many lives. The windows were replaced by new brick which can be seen at the right-hand side of the house. Since the war the Fogg family have fed and watered walkers and cyclists who were always made welcome. Caddies from Stockport Golf Club have now made the house their regular watering hole.

The OldKnow Toll House, built around 1797, was used to collect tolls for the use of the new turnpike road from Dan Bank to Offerton Fold. This road was specially built by Samuel Oldknow to recoup some of the obvious expense he had incurred upgrading a packhorse trail into a decent roadway. This also included the building of two substantial bridges.

During the 1980s an enterprising Marple gentleman built a model of the 1797 Toll House.

In the 1990s the model appeared in a charity shop window. I subsequently bought it and furnished it in the style it might have been in the mid-1800s.

A view taken of the model's interior. When Mrs De-Bartard lived here she sold glasses of orange juice to travellers.

Highfield House stood high above the Offerton fields on Bean Leach Road. Built by Thomas Wilson, no relation to the Hough-Wilsons, he owned the Foggbrook mill which he opened as a bleaching and dyeing works. The house had a vinery and stables as well as kennels for his dogs. Mr Wilson was a keen hunting man and kept gun dogs, which he buried in a small pet graveyard in the garden area.

Bosden House is a Dodge house, which does not immediately proclaim its history. The picture gives an impression of a purely Victorian background. The house is actually built on the foundations of a very old Dodge House.

Known as the Clock House this building adjoins the main house and can be seen from Offerton Road. This would have been built at the same time as the Victorian house and serves as stables etc.

Bosden House, Offerton Road. Built on a hillside overlooking Offerton, A high-walled garden slopes away at the side of the house. Coming from the garden the cellar can be entered at the floor level. One immediately notices the original stone foundations of the house. Stone-mullion windows as far as the first floor give a hint of its much earlier origins.

Entering the cellar you see an immaculate brick-vaulted ceiling, and an ancient stone-mullion window covered in many years ago. Stone flagg seats encircle the area.

The gatehouse, Woodlands Lodge, at the end of the 500 yard-long driveway to Woodlands House. Today this house still stands as a relic of the past on the edge of Offerton Lane.

Opposite above: To the right of the cellar door is a slop stone. An ancient pump to an artesian well deep underground supplies water for washing for this household.

Opposite below: Woodlands, a three-storey Georgian mansion which stood overlooking the extensive lower Goyt Valley and river flood plains. For some years Mr Ramsden owned the house and the woodlands behind and I recall in my youth referring to Ramsden's Woods. He also owned the area now used by Offerton Cricket Club. The club still calls the area 'The Paddock' as Mr Ramsden would exercise race horses that he owned there.

—LISBURNE HOTEL—

These old stone cottages stood on Dooley Lane for centuries. They were immediately next to the Hare and Hounds public house. They were eventually knocked down to re-route the line of the road around the back of the pub, and today the area is the pub car park.

Opposite above: This corner of Offerton depicts a shop at the corner of Garth Road and Hempshaw Lane. The photograph was taken at the time of the great fire at Battersby's hat works, which was right opposite. Here, an obvious clean-up operation is in progress.

Opposite below: Built in the early 1800s, Lisburn House was the home of Jonathan Bradley. No photographs ever came to light whilst researching its history, the only record was this line drawing made for a calendar. Over the years the house had been a maternity home and a hotel. Finally demolished, a block of flats called Shawcross Fold now occupies the site of the old house.

The old and the new. The final photograph in this chapter contains buildings with a wide range of ages. They range from 1765 for the White Houses (centre distance), then working to the right, the terraced pair date from about 1850. The old Midway House pub dates from the mid-1700s. Then we get to the more modern architect-designed semi from 1930s. Moving over to the left-hand side of the photograph, the mix of modern detached houses presents a pleasant and homely façade along the main road. Such is the quality of this 1935 photograph that the registration plate on the soft-topped vehicle outside the pub can be read with a magnifier– NE – which I believe makes it a Manchester-registered vehicle.

four

Churches,
Schools &
Events

St John's Church School was built in 1876 and paid for by public subscription at a cost of £950. This building catered for the educational and religious needs of the children of Offerton. Despite the addition of several annexes over the years, it eventually became surplus to requirements and was demolished during the 1980s.

A proliferation of flowers on the inside of St John's Church School indicates a harvest festival, c. 1920. Long tip-up desks with grooves for ink pens and holes for inkpot wells remind the older reader of early schooldays. In the corner stands an old pedal organ and close by is the collection plate.

St John's Church School fancy dress day, the year being around 1925. The theme was nursery rhyme characters. This photograph, provided by the Queen of Hearts some seventy-five years later, shows the group in the playground. Ormes Farm is in the background.

The skeletal framework of the new St John's church rises in 1969, blotting out a view of the old church behind.

The Offerton Weslyan Chapel was built in 1887. Now known as Offerton Methodist Chapel it shares the Methodist teaching with the more modern building on Dialstone Lane.

The annual church walks from Offerton, the church banner leading the way. In earlier days the walks were led by the Sunday school superintendent, traditional brass band and the scholars and parishioners.

Rose Queen Brenda Hogg leads her retinue of Sunday school scholars from Offerton Methodist Chapel. In the background is the Lisburn Lane and Marple Road junction. The Golden Hind public house today stands where the old Dodgefold cottages were, on the right of the photograph.

Rosebud Queen Helen Preston and retinue anticipate the photographer's bidding to smile.

Above and below: At two separate crowning ceremonies, the girls and boys, on a very crowded stage, eagerly await the moment of the official crowning of the Rose Queens. of Offerton Methodist Chapel.

The local school field is utilized for the festivities and is where, after the official crowning, games and competitions take place.

Eager young cub-scouts assist Martyn Preston and Philip Bowden (with the spades) as they plant a Christmas tree outside the newly built cub hut.

Opposite above: The Union Chapel, Littlemoor. Opened on 7 June 1872, this non-conformist chapel cost £1,200. The land was given by Charles Earnshaw and the foundation stone was laid by Sir James Watt of Abney Hall. It was built in Gothic style with a square tower and a packsaddle roof. The leanings towards non-conformity failed and an application was made for funds from the Cheshire Union. Closing and joining the United Reform, the congregation moved to the old Banks Lane School. The church was eventually demolished and the land now serves as a car park for the Gardeners Arms public house, Little Street.

Opposite below: A plot of land was purchased from Mr and Mrs Moorhouse who lived at Woodlands and owned the estate, in order to build St Alban's parish church. The estimated cost of building the new church was £6,000. The church was consecrated on 12 December 1899 and the first vicar was the Revd Gilbertson. The first organist and choirmaster was Walter Battersby of hat-making fame. The original design was to include a spire which would naturally have held a bell. The bell was eventually hung on the outside of the church high on the gable end. A fundraising effort after the Second World War was put towards the erection of a useful building which was named the Galilee. This was built onto the west end of the church.

Chadkirk Chapel.

The chapel's walled garden provides an idyllic setting in Spring 2004. Times were when this garden provided a wealth of sustenance, including herbs, for those in and around the ancient chapel. The Friends of Chadkirk are responsible for the continued work in these beautiful gardens.

Offerton Boys Industrial School was built in 1897. The purpose of the school was to train and educate wayward boys, which rather unfairly included orphans, to a better way of life. It cost £20,000 to build and was a follow-up to the ragged school, which was established in the town in 1854 and was run by a committee of volunteers.

A more recent photograph of the Industrial School shows what a fine building this was. In 1950 it was taken over by the Health Authority and used to house and cater for disabled people. Those more able worked in the occupational therapy department and in the extensive gardens. A special hydrotherapy pool was built for the especial use of the residents. When the main building was demolished, the pool was retained to carry on the very important therapy work.

The Girls Industrial School was built on Dialstone Lane to house and educate unfortunate girls. In later years it was purchased by the Battersby Hat Co. who utilized it as a social club for its workforce. At the end of the Second World War it was requisitioned by the Ministry as a tax office. It was then bought by the Lukic family and turned into a hotel named the Belgrade, which later become the Britannia.

In the 1950s the Girls Industrial School made an imposing silhouette against the backdrop of a sunset.

This fine, detailed photograph shows Dialstone Central School as it was in the late 1950s. Built in a traditional E-shape in 1938, the quadrangle and playground were positioned at the right-hand side. As the school became more popular in the 1960s, prefabricated buildings were added. The school was situated on the edge of the countryside, with Shaws Farm (Lisburn Farm) in the top right-hand corner of the photograph, awakening memories for many of the ice cream parlour and milkshakes to be had there after school. Lisburn Lane was still a country hedge-lined path, with a stile going off to Whistle Hollow. The pond held every kind of newt imaginable and Lapwings nested in the fields around us.

Dialstone Central School class photograph, 1946. At this time the headmaster was Mr Leslie Raisbeck.

This aerial photograph of Stockport Technical School, which was built in 1936, shows some of the historic buildings that were in the area at the time of this photograph. The bottom left depicts the ancient Mile End Hall in process of demolition. Above and to the right is the much-lamented lost Blue Lagoon swimming pool.

Named the Goyt Bank High School for Girls when first opened, it was eventually re-named Offerton High School (mixed). Another school set on the edge of the countryside, the Goyt River lay behind, shrouded by magnificent woodlands, the Ramsdens and Ashtons, as we knew them in our boyhood. A well-defined path can still be seen in this photograph, although bureaucratic intervention prevented the locals from convenient access to these beautiful woodlands.

Above: Offerton Hall Infants School was built in the 1970s to accommodate the children of the new neighbourhood unit built on the green fields of Offerton. A commanding view over the Poise Brook Valley on a frosty morning portrays a little of this magnificent landscape.

Left: A pair of fine Victorian gateposts marked the entrance to this fine private school. During the 1930/40s Lymefield School was run by the very well respected Misses Lee, and the pupils here were guaranteed a very high standard of education.

Above: Well-dressing at Chadkirk, 1999. One regular event to raise funds for the Stockport Heritage Trust was a festival weekend celebrating ancient well-dressing. The flower-bedecked picture stands over the famous well of St Chad, who is reputed to have settled in Offerton in the sixth century, teaching Christianity.

Opposite above: For ten years an annual May Day festival was held on the village green at Offerton. The green had been donated to the people of Offerton by landowner Tom Whitely in the early 1900s. The Offerton Community Council organized stalls and sideshows, and the main features were the morris dancers and the Offerton clog dancers.

Opposite below: Maypole dancers from a local school with a backdrop of surrounding houses; at the festival the green echoed with music.

Above and below: Over the years re-enactments have taken place on the green sward in front of the historic chapel. In one such epic, Roman soldiers set up a marching camp and challenged neighbours to fight with swords.

Opposite above: Another very significant event was the cavalcade of horse-drawn vehicles celebrating the 200 years since the turnpike road – Marple Road – was opened through Offerton. The builder, Samuel Oldknow, would have been justly proud to have seen this bicentenary celebration. The occasion was marked by the Mayor of Stockport, Cllr Malcolm Lowe, in the first carriage, while local schoolchildren rode in the other vehicles.

Opposite below: Unfortunately, a highwayman, reputed to have R.T. engraved on his flintlock, held up the coach and demanded, 'Your money or your life'. The author, a devout coward, handed over a leather purse to Mr T but, on learning that the gold coins were for the Mayor's charity, Mr T generously handed them back.

Dated 1889, this quality plate photograph is of a church outing. A bell tower can be seen above the roof of the house behind. Everyone is dressed in their Sunday best, with the ladies in bonnets and shawls and the gentlemen in their customary bowlers. The photographer resided at 20 Dialstone Lane.

Opposite above: A coal mine deep under Poynton belonging to Lord Vernon. The seam shelved upwards under Hazel Grove and close to the surface in Offerton. Many years ago it was, for a short while, uncovered. This 4ft-deep seam of high-quality coal was only broken by the River Goyt, after which it carried on through under Bredbury and Hyde.

Opposite below: This massive stone was excavated from the gravel beds under Offerton. In the 1950s a competition was organised to guess the weight; it turned out to weigh 1.5 tons. The name of the winner is not recorded.

Shortly before the old church school of St John's was demolished, the author received permission from the church authorities to search for the foundation stone that had been laid by Mrs Bradshaw-Isherwood of Marple Hall. History books recorded the fact that coins and artefacts had been placed within the stone in 1876.

Sure enough, the artefacts were found and displayed. They included a half-crown, a florin and a three-penny piece, all of solid silver. There was also one penny and two half-pennies. All the coins were from 1876, the era of Queen Victoria, and in mint condition. The newspapers and programme from the day had been badly damaged by water over the 113 years they had lain within the stone.

five

Farms

Top o' the Green Farm is an impressive timber-framed fifteenth-century building which is grade II listed. Strangely enough very little of the building's early history is actually known. The house commands a breath-taking view across the Goyt Valley and, if those old timbers could speak, who knows what they have seen approaching from Werneth and Bredbury? It is believed that the Sutton family planted the six magnificent oaks which stand in front of the house.

A more recent photograph of Top o' the Green Farm taken by the author in the 1970s. Some landscaping has taken place since then.

A sad and dilapidated Yew Tree Farm now lies empty and scorched. Jack Sutton worked the farm as long as I can remember, well over fifty years, but before this, in the early years of the twentieth century, the farm was occupied by Thomas Kay, an industrial chemist famous for Kay's firelighters and flypapers. A lover of good music, he founded a trust still operating today which provided money towards the musical education of gifted young people. I was fortunate enough to win a three-year singing scholarship, which set me off on sixty years of music.

I have spent hundreds of hours in Kay's Wood watching and filming birds and animals deep in the woods, and now have 400ft of cine film on what now are quite rare birds and animals, including willow tits, sparrow hawks, weasels and many more.

The late Ann Cross, an Offerton historian, asked me to take a photograph of the yew tree at the farm of the same name. Today this tree is considerably larger.

A manor house has occupied this site in Offerton since the twelfth century. Today Offerton Hall Farm, a stately, many-gabled house, stands here. At one time this was a moated building occupied by the de Offertons. The male line failed and an heiress married into the Winningtons. In the 1600s we suspect the timber-framed original hall was demolished and the house as we see it today was built. The imposing façade and studded front door is to the right, facing north-west towards Stockport.

Opposite above: The well-worn path from Yew Tree Farm leading over a stile, down to the woods and across to Hawk Green. The five-bar gate leans at a drunken angle and through it is the overgrown farmyard which once rang with the sound of people pitch-forking hay into the loft above the shippons. No sign now of the swallows that came every year to nest.

Opposite below: The view from the path towards the woodlands where Jack Sutton once pointed out the patterns on the top meadow. This undulating appearance in the grass is leftover from the medieval method of ploughing.

Another very popular afternoon outing was to this ancient monument close to Broad Oak Farm. This moat-like lake surrounded a mound of earth which had been the site of an archaeological dig in the 1920s but required further excavation. In the meanwhile paddle boats could be hired for a few pence for rides round the lake.

Opposite above: This very early postcard shows a tree-less area around Offerton Hall Farm and its barn. The barn itself pre-dates the house by many years. Cromwell's soldiers and horses are reputed to have utilized the barn whilst they were in the area.

Opposite below: Known locally as Shaw's Farm, Lisburn Farm is overshadowed from the back by Lisburn House. Peter Shaw's farm was very popular locally for its duck pond and ice cream. Peter, a very small man could often be seen scurrying about the farm in his gumboots when most people were buying a milkshake or delicious ice cream from the parlour across the road next to the school gates. A regular Sunday afternoon walk with an ice cream took you down the hedge-lined Lisburn Lane, over the stile to Whistle Hollow and across to Bean Leach.

Situated on the winding road from Hazel Grove, Bean Leach Farm stands with its gabled end to the road. It was demolished in the 1970s to make way for the Offerton Green development and the access road, Shearwater Road. The large tree to the left of the farm survived and is still there today.

Lower Dan Bank Farm is certainly a unique building, hidden away behind the trees along Dan Bank. The farm is a castellated building, along with the barns. The old horse-drawn hay cart and the laborious method of hay storage brings back memories of sweating, aching bodies after a long day under the blazing sun of long-gone summers.

Above: Old Manor Farm is an immaculately preserved house set high above the Dan Bank. It is certainly one of the best examples in the area of timber-framing, dating from the fifteenth century or earlier.

Left: Massive cruck frames throughout Old Manor Farm support roof beams of great proportions. The whole house is tastefully fitted out.

The aptly-named Windy Ridge Farm is another building poised on the edge of the valley. Today it has much improved in appearance from its old farming days when it was the home of Thomas Whitely.

The Fold, with its natural pebbled walkway between Harvey's Farm and the cottages. The cottages date back to the sixteenth century, with wattle and daub walls, and box-framed interiors. A previous era was discovered when entering the roof space; a complete new slate roof had at some time been built over. It must have proved easier to build over than dismantle the lower roof. The last family to work the farm were the Harveys. I went to school with the youngest, Peter Harvey.

six

Views

The past and the present. This pair of magnificent shire horses plod their way across an Offerton field whilst in the background a diesel tractor noisily does the same job.

In a buttercup-strewn field off Bean Leach Road, this mare and her foal enjoy the spring sunshine of 1960. Bean Leach Road and the farm can be seen in the background.

Above and below: These two photographs of Ashton's Woods were taken from the same position show nature at its extremes, winter and spring. Above, the gaunt skeletal tree branches reach upwards, whilst below, the warm spring sunshine encourages the bluebells to raise their heads skywards.

Offerton village green in 1960 protected by a covering of snow, while grey skies presage more on the way.

Icicles hang majestically from the massive sandstone escarpment above the Poise Brook.

This bend in the Poise Brook is known locally as Fossil Creek. Erosion of the stream bank has over many years exposed the end of an ancient coal seam. Children collect fossils from the carboniferous shale depicting fronds of fern leaves. Wild animals and birds abound in these woods, and the tracks of a fox can be seen in the snow in the foreground. A recent February bird-count recorded twenty-three species.

An early spring morning captured on film as the mist clears from above the stream. Two new bridges and a newly designated footpath lead from Holiday Lane to the bridge over the River Goyt.

This fine sandstone bridge dated 1690 was designed and built by Henry Watson. The bridge was commissioned by Henry Bradshaw VI. A sandstone block gives details of the history under the bridge structure.

Opposite above: This picture speaks for itself, with the quiet waters of the Goyt at Otterspool Bridge slipping past the beautiful cottages on its bank, each complementing the other.

Opposite below: In my younger days these woodlands were called Ashton's Woods, named after the farmer to whom they belonged. This path is a continuation of Holiday Lane, making a very pleasant walk to the river.

Looking down from the Marple Road, the massive flood plain of the Goyt Valley is spread before you. The Goyt enters Offerton and lower Bredbury from Marple Dale. Meandering between tree-lined sandy banks it eventually enters Woodbank and flows into Stockport where its confluence forms the River Mersey. This area of Offerton holds the secret of where exactly the Romans crossed. Was it at Broadford – a pebbly shallow in Offerton only used occasionally by farm vehicles – or higher upriver at Marple Dale? Broadford is my guess, as this lines up with Bongs Lane. The skyline from the left spreads from Stockport round to Bredbury. The Offerton Sand and Gravel works can be seen left of the photograph whilst Bongs Farm lies centre-left. To the right is the sewage farm and the tree-shrouded Middle Farm at Lower Bredbury.

Jim Fearnley Bridge. Jim Fearnley worked for many years as a warden for the Etherow and Goyt Valley. The area he covered went far downriver and through Offerton. One day, by the river he saw an opportunity to build a bridge for the people of Offerton to cross the River Goyt, something they had never before been able to do. This would join up with paths to Stockport, Bredbury, Marple and beyond. Along with other valley wardens this bridge was built close to the Poise Brook confluence. This was virtually the centre of Offerton. Unfortunately we only used this access for a short time as the central point from Offerton was closed to us – something we intend to alter.

Opposite above: This narrowing flood plain along the Poise Brook at Bean Leach passes under the Foggbrook Bridge at Marple Road. Over sixty years I have seen this area turned into a massive lake of floodwater.

Opposite below: The end of the line brings us to a modern innovation beloved of children and adults. Set in a corner of Offerton, the Wyevale Garden Centre was opened in 1983. It took over a market garden which had been operated on this spot for many years by Mr Ridgeway of Romiley. I recall rows of saplings both there and on the other side of the river. I believe the ground was rented from the church. Wyevale have expanded over the years and now this garden centre has established itself as a pleasant and hospitable venue for the whole family.

Other local titles published by Tempus

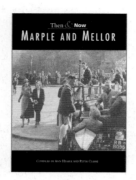

Marple and Mellor: Then & Now
ANN HEARLE AND PETER CLARKE

In this book over 90 archive photographs have been carefully matched with photographs of the same scenes taken today. Most of the early pictures, taken in the first years of the twentieth century, show every aspect of life in the area: street scenes, churches, schools, celebrations, industries, farms and shops. It is a visual record of communities leading very different lives in much altered conditions to those of today.

0 7524 2644 3

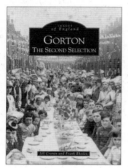

Gorton: The Second Selection
JILL CRONIN AND FRANK RHODES

A collection of over 220 archive photographs, taking a look at some of the changes in leisure, housing, business and industry which have taken place over the last century in Gorton. A nostalgic look back at the pubs, cinemas, churches and schools that have changed over the years, including poignant photographs of VE Day street party celebrations. Each picture is supported by a wealth of historical detail sure to appeal to all who know, or have known, Gorton.

0 7524 2669 9

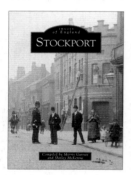

Stockport
MORRIS GARRATT AND SHIRLEY MCKENNA

This detailed collection of 220 photographs and illustrations, many never published before, takes in the sights and scenes of Stockport and other surrounding areas, including Vernon Park, Portwood, Tiviot Dale, the Heatons and Edgeley. The reader will encounter townscapes, streets and buildings such as pubs, cinemas and shops, many of which have now disappeared. These images will awaken memories among older residents, while showing younger readers the face of the town as it used to be.

0 7524 1128 4

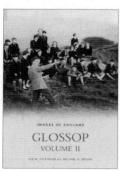

Glossop: Volume II
SUE HICKINSON AND MICHAEL H. BROWN

This collection of over 200 images portrays life in and around the Derbyshire town of Glossop over the last 100 years. There were many photographic studios in the area producing picture postcards featuring idyllic rural scenes, mills, shops, civic events and celebrations. Accompanied by informative captions, this volume will delight all those who have lived and worked in the area, or who have spent time exploring the valleys and dales of this intriguing part of Derbyshire.

0 7524 3286 9

If you are interested in purchasing other books published by Tempus, or in case you have difficulty finding any Tempus books in your local bookshop, you can also place orders directly through our website

www.tempus-publishing.com